To Harry Bartlett

Three Designs for Three Timpani

Robert Muczynski
Op. 11, No. 2

I

II

Allegretto (waltz-like; with grace) ♩. = 50
F-C-F
pp
p
poco
f
fp (non cresc.)
f
fp
marc.
p
p sub.
ff
sempre p
ff sub.
mf
poco a poco rit.
pp
Change to F-B♭-E♭

III

Moderato (Starting slowly from rim to center and accelerating until Allegro molto)
Allegro molto ♩= 154
F-B♭-E♭
pp
f ben ritmato con precisione
ff
sf
fp
poco
mf
p
f
slower and slower
(near rim; dampen with L.H. fingers)
quite slow
rit. molto
Allegro
undampen
p (R) (R) sim.
pp
sec.
sff sub.